12-11

POETRY FOR CHILDREN

Bed in Summer

By Robert Louis Stevenson
Illustrated by Jesse Reisch

Distributed by The Child's World®
1980 Lookout Drive • Mankato, MN 56003-1705
800-599-READ • www.childsworld.com

Acknowledgments
The Child's World®: Mary Berendes, Publishing Director
The Design Lab: Kathleen Petelinsek, Design

Library of Congress Cataloging-in-Publication Data
Stevenson, Robert Louis, 1850–1894.
  Bed in summer / by Robert Louis Stevenson ; illustrated by Jesse Reisch.
    p. cm.
  ISBN 978-1-60973-151-9 (library reinforced : alk. paper)
  I. Reisch, Jesse, ill. II. Title.
  PR5489.B43 2011
  821'.8—dc22   2011004997

Printed in the United States of America in Mankato, Minnesota.
July 2011
PA02091

In winter I get up at night ...

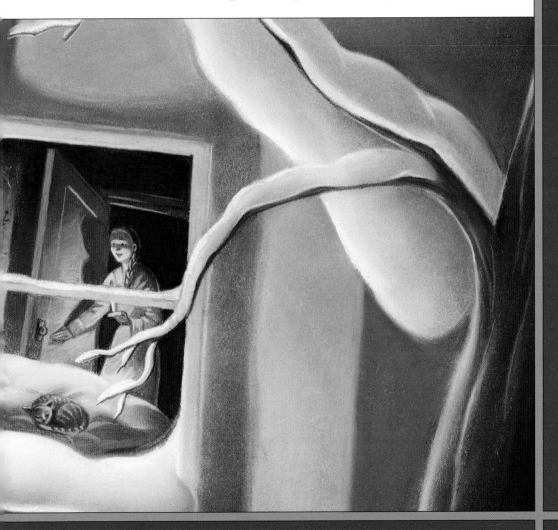

and dress by yellow candle-light.

In summer, quite the other way,
I have to go to bed by day.

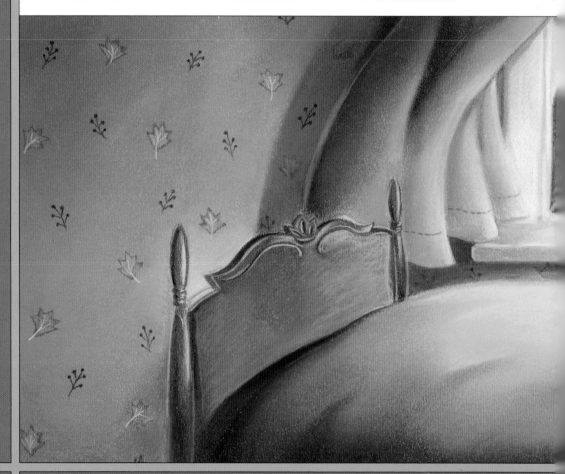

I have to go to bed and see
the birds still hopping on the tree.

Or hear the grown-up
people's feet . . .

still going past me in the street.

And does it not seem hard to you,
when all the sky is clear and blue,

and I should like so much to play,

to have to go to bed by day?

Bed in Summer

In winter I get up at night
And dress by yellow candle-light.
In summer, quite the other way,
I have to go to bed by day.

I have to go to bed and see
The birds still hopping on the tree,
Or hear the grown-up people's feet
Still going past me in the street.

And does it not seem hard to you,
When all the sky is clear and blue,
And I should like so much to play,
To have to go to bed by day?

—*Robert Louis Stevenson*

What makes a poem a poem?

With just a few words, a poem can make you feel things in a flash. It delights you, amazes you. It makes you laugh out loud or shed a tear. You know a poem is successful when it tickles your brain or touches your heart.

Poets choose their words very carefully. They don't just think about what words *mean*. They think about how they *sound*. Why write "sticky mess," when "mashed marshmallow" is so much more fun to say? Those repeating *m* sounds? They're alliteration in action!

Poets surprise you with similes and metaphors. A school hallway becomes a pirate's plank. A bed flies away in a dream. In this way, poets make their words come alive. A poem about a campfire makes you wrinkle your nose. A poem about a slithering snake makes you squirm in your seat.

Poets have all kinds of tools and tricks to make their work come alive. Maybe it's a rhyming verse. Maybe it's the rhythm of repeated sounds. Maybe it's the imagery of a melting ice cream cone. With the tricks of the trade, anything can become a poem!

About the Author

Robert Louis Stevenson was a famous writer and poet. He was born in Scotland in 1850. He was often sick as a child, and began to write stories to occupy his time. Stevenson is best known for writing the stories *Treasure Island, Kidnapped,* and *The Strange Case of Dr. Jekyll and Mr. Hyde.* Robert Louis Stevenson died in 1894.

About the Illustrator

Jesse Reisch grew up in the midwest, studied art in Chicago, lived in Europe, India, and San Francisco, and now happily resides in her casita in San Miguel de Allende, Mexico. Recently, her interest expanded to children's books, which gives her inner child much delight.